The
Entrepreneur's
Success
Journal

Mind, Body & Money

by:
Candice Ellis, MBA, MHPrac

The
Entrepreneur's
Success
Journal

Mind, Body & Money

by:
Candice Ellis, MBA, MHPrac

Purpose: Self care mixed with Business care. This journal was created as a resource for entrepreneurs. My goal is for you to be wholistically successful: mentally, physically and financially. Each impacts your stress level, productivity and accomplishments. This journal provides keys to not only organize your tasks, check things off your list, journal your thoughts and ideas but also provides practical tools. There are breathing techniques, calendars, business reminders and inspiration all throughout to aide in your life and business success.

Entrepreneur's

Journal

Mind, Body & Money

by:
Candice Ellis, MBA, MHPrac

The
Entrepreneur's
Success
Journal

Mind, Body & Money

by:
Candice Ellis, MBA, MHPrac

Resource guide:

Breathing:
https://www.uofmhealth.org/health-library/uz2255
https://www.medicalnewstoday.com/articles/324417#apps

Quotes:
https://www.briantracy.com/blog/personal-success/26-motivational-quotes-for-success/

The Entrepreneur's Success Journal

You are unstoppable!

This means you have the power to be consistent, the grit to endure whatever comes your way and the stamina to obtain the goals you set forth for yourself. This is NOT a label to dehumanize you but to assure you that you can PUSH through whatever comes your way. Yes, at times you will get tired. Yes, you may feel like giving up. Yes, you may not feel like continuing. But guess what- YOU GOT THIS! Allow yourself GRACE to REST so that you can keep going. REST and SELF-CARE keeps you unstoppable so that you can continue to pour into people and the things you LOVE.

Breathe:

Intro:

Try this exercise when you first get up in the morning to relieve muscle stiffness and clear clogged breathing passages. Then use it throughout the day to relieve back tension.

Instructions:

1. From a standing position, bend forward from the waist with your knees slightly bent, letting your arms dangle close to the floor.
2. As you inhale slowly and deeply, return to a standing position by rolling up slowing, lifting your head last.
3. Hold your breath for just a few seconds in this standing position.
4. Exhale slowly as you return to the original position, bending forward from the waist.

Introspect:

Notice how you feel at the end of the exercise.

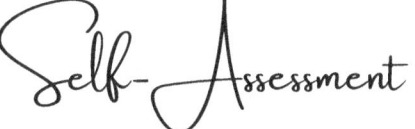

Goal Setting for
____ Quarter

What are 3 areas that you want to grow in personally?

_____
_____
_____
_____
_____
_____
_____
_____
_____

What is your end goal for all three goals?

_____
_____
_____
_____
_____
_____
_____

How committed are you to your goals?

_____
_____
_____
_____
_____
_____
_____

1st Goal

Steps to achieving my Goal   **Priorities**

Quote of the Day

*"You Learn More From Failure Than
From Success. Don't Let It Stop You.
Failure Builds Character."*
– Anonymous

2nd Goal

_____

Steps to achieving my Goal   **Priorities**

Quote of the Day

"If You Are Working On Something That
You Really Care About, You Don't Have
To Be Pushed. The Vision Pulls You."
– Steve Jobs

3rd Goal

_____

Steps to achieving my Goal   **Priorities**

Quote of the Day

*"People Who Are Crazy Enough To Think
They Can Change The World, Are The
Ones Who Do."
– Rob Siltanen*

Business Goals for _____ Quarter

Marketing: How much time and money will you invest?

Followup: What customers and partners do you need to reachout to?

Tasks: What are the tasks you are avoiding but need to get done?

Complete: What did you finish this quarter? (Roll any unfinished task to next quarter.)

Weekly
SCHEDULE
PLANNER

MONTH

WEEK NO.

MONDAY

TUESDAY

WEDNESDAY

THURSDAY

FRIDAY

SATURDAY

SUNDAY

NOTES

Weekly
SCHEDULE
PLANNER

MONTH

WEEK NO.

MONDAY

TUESDAY

WEDNESDAY

THURSDAY

FRIDAY

SATURDAY

SUNDAY

NOTES

Weekly
SCHEDULE
PLANNER

MONDAY

TUESDAY

MONTH

WEEK NO.

WEDNESDAY

THURSDAY

FRIDAY

SATURDAY

SUNDAY

NOTES

Weekly
SCHEDULE
PLANNER

MONTH

WEEK NO.

MONDAY

TUESDAY

WEDNESDAY

THURSDAY

FRIDAY

SATURDAY

SUNDAY

NOTES

Weekly
SCHEDULE
PLANNER

MONTH

WEEK NO.

MONDAY

TUESDAY

WEDNESDAY

THURSDAY

FRIDAY

SATURDAY

SUNDAY

NOTES

How are You doing?

Mind:

_____
_____
_____
_____

Body:

_____
_____
_____
_____
_____
_____

Money:

_____
_____
_____
_____
_____
_____

Set Your Intentions:

_____
_____
_____
_____
_____
_____

Journaled
Thoughts...

_____
_____
_____
_____
_____
_____
_____
_____
_____
_____
_____
_____
_____
_____
_____
_____
_____
_____
_____
_____
_____
_____
_____
_____
_____
_____
_____
_____

Accomplished

Goals for the Month

Month: _____

_____
_____
_____
_____
_____
_____
_____
_____
_____
_____
_____
_____
_____
_____
_____
_____
_____
_____
_____
_____
_____
_____
_____
_____
_____
_____
_____
_____
_____
_____
_____
_____
_____
_____

Weekly
SCHEDULE
PLANNER

MONDAY

TUESDAY

MONTH

WEEK NO.

WEDNESDAY

THURSDAY

FRIDAY

SATURDAY

SUNDAY

NOTES

Weekly
SCHEDULE
PLANNER

MONTH

WEEK NO.

MONDAY

TUESDAY

WEDNESDAY

THURSDAY

FRIDAY

SATURDAY

SUNDAY

NOTES

*W*eekly
SCHEDULE
PLANNER

MONDAY

TUESDAY

MONTH

WEEK NO.

WEDNESDAY

THURSDAY

FRIDAY

SATURDAY

SUNDAY

NOTES

Weekly
SCHEDULE
PLANNER

MONTH

WEEK NO.

MONDAY

TUESDAY

WEDNESDAY

THURSDAY

FRIDAY

SATURDAY

SUNDAY

NOTES

Weekly
SCHEDULE
PLANNER

MONDAY

TUESDAY

MONTH

WEEK NO.

WEDNESDAY

THURSDAY

FRIDAY

SATURDAY

SUNDAY

NOTES

How are You doing?

Mind:

_____
_____
_____
_____

Body:

_____
_____
_____
_____
_____

Money:

_____
_____
_____
_____
_____

Set Your Intentions:

_____
_____
_____
_____
_____

Journaled

Thoughts...

Accomplished

Goals for the Month

Month: _____

_____
_____
_____
_____
_____
_____
_____
_____
_____
_____
_____
_____
_____
_____
_____
_____
_____
_____
_____
_____
_____
_____
_____
_____
_____
_____
_____
_____
_____
_____
_____
_____

Weekly
SCHEDULE
PLANNER

MONTH

WEEK NO.

MONDAY

TUESDAY

WEDNESDAY

THURSDAY

FRIDAY

SATURDAY

SUNDAY

NOTES

Weekly
SCHEDULE
PLANNER

MONDAY

TUESDAY

MONTH

WEEK NO.

WEDNESDAY

THURSDAY

FRIDAY

SATURDAY

SUNDAY

NOTES

Weekly
SCHEDULE
PLANNER

MONTH

WEEK NO.

MONDAY

TUESDAY

WEDNESDAY

THURSDAY

FRIDAY

SATURDAY

SUNDAY

NOTES

Weekly
SCHEDULE
PLANNER

MONDAY

TUESDAY

MONTH

WEEK NO.

WEDNESDAY

THURSDAY

FRIDAY

SATURDAY

SUNDAY

NOTES

Weekly
SCHEDULE
PLANNER

MONDAY

TUESDAY

MONTH

WEEK NO.

WEDNESDAY

THURSDAY

FRIDAY

SATURDAY

SUNDAY

NOTES

How are You doing?

Mind:

_____
_____
_____
_____

Body:

_____
_____
_____
_____
_____
_____

Money:

_____
_____
_____
_____
_____
_____

Set Your Intentions:

_____
_____
_____
_____
_____
_____

Journaled
Thoughts...

Accomplished
Goals for the
previous Quarter

Quarter/Year: _____

_____
_____
_____
_____
_____
_____
_____
_____
_____
_____
_____
_____
_____
_____
_____
_____
_____
_____
_____
_____
_____
_____
_____
_____
_____
_____
_____
_____
_____
_____
_____
_____
_____
_____
_____

The
Entrepreneur's

Success

Journal

Life is what you make it!

Being an entrepreneur, living with purpose, and making your own money are all beautiful things! Entrepreneurship requires much of your time, but there are also benefits of being your own boss such as freedom to enjoy family, self-care, rest and/or just overall personal enjoyment. Therefore, I would encourage you to make "Time Freedom" a goal. As you are working to achieve that goal – do not forget to smell the flowers, laugh, be MINDFUL and enjoy yourself along the way. Do not allow the beauty of life to be robbed due to the demands of entrepreneurship.

Breathe:

Intro:

Belly breathing is easy to do and very relaxing. Try this basic exercise anytime you need to relax or relieve stress.

Instructions:

1. Sit or lie flat in a comfortable position.
2. Put one hand on your belly just below your ribs and the other hand on your chest.
3. Take a deep breath in through your nose, and let your belly push your hand out. Your chest should not move.
4. Breathe out through pursed lips as if you were whistling. Feel the hand on your belly go in, and use it to push all the air out.
5. Do this breathing 3 to 10 times. Take your time with each breath.

Introspect:

Notice how you feel at the end of the exercise.

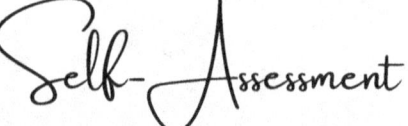

Goal Setting for
_____ Quarter

What are 3 areas that you want to grow in personally?

_____
_____
_____
_____
_____
_____
_____
_____
_____

What is your end goal for all three goals?

_____
_____
_____
_____
_____
_____
_____

How committed are you to your goals?

_____
_____
_____
_____
_____
_____
_____

1st Goal

Steps to achieving my Goal   **Priorities**

Quote of the Day

"It doesn't matter what you're trying to accomplish. It's all a matter of discipline... I was determined to discover what life held for me beyond the inner-city streets."
– Wilma Rudolph

2nd Goal

_____

Steps to achieving my Goal   **Priorities**

Quote of the Day

"The key to success is to keep growing in all areas of life-mental, emotional, spiritual, as well as physical."
– Julius Erving

3rd Goal

Steps to achieving my Goal   **Priorities**

Quote of the Day

*"The will to win, the desire to succeed,
the urge to reach your full
potential...these are the keys that will
unlock the door to personal excellence."
– Eddie Robinson*

Business Goals for _____ Quarter

Marketing: How much time and money will you invest?

Followup: What customers and partners do you need to reachout to?

Tasks: What are the tasks you are avoiding but need to get done?

Complete: What did you finish this quarter? (Roll any unfinished task to next quarter.)

Weekly
SCHEDULE
PLANNER

MONTH

WEEK NO.

MONDAY

TUESDAY

WEDNESDAY

THURSDAY

FRIDAY

SATURDAY

SUNDAY

NOTES

Weekly
SCHEDULE
PLANNER

MONTH

WEEK NO.

MONDAY

TUESDAY

WEDNESDAY

THURSDAY

FRIDAY

SATURDAY

SUNDAY

NOTES

Weekly
SCHEDULE
PLANNER

MONDAY

TUESDAY

MONTH

WEEK NO.

WEDNESDAY

THURSDAY

FRIDAY

SATURDAY

SUNDAY

NOTES

Weekly
SCHEDULE
PLANNER

MONDAY

TUESDAY

MONTH

WEEK NO.

WEDNESDAY

THURSDAY

FRIDAY

SATURDAY

SUNDAY

NOTES

Weekly
SCHEDULE
PLANNER

MONTH

WEEK NO.

MONDAY

TUESDAY

WEDNESDAY

THURSDAY

FRIDAY

SATURDAY

SUNDAY

NOTES

How are You doing?

Mind:

_____
_____
_____
_____
_____

Body:

_____
_____
_____
_____
_____
_____
_____

Money:

_____
_____
_____
_____
_____
_____
_____

Set Your Intentions:

_____
_____
_____
_____
_____
_____
_____

Journaled
Thoughts...

Goals for the Month

Month: _____

_____
_____
_____
_____
_____
_____
_____
_____
_____
_____
_____
_____
_____
_____
_____
_____
_____
_____
_____
_____
_____
_____
_____
_____
_____
_____
_____
_____
_____

Weekly
SCHEDULE
PLANNER

MONTH

WEEK NO.

MONDAY

TUESDAY

WEDNESDAY

THURSDAY

FRIDAY

SATURDAY

SUNDAY

NOTES

Weekly
SCHEDULE
PLANNER

MONTH

WEEK NO.

MONDAY

TUESDAY

WEDNESDAY

THURSDAY

FRIDAY

SATURDAY

SUNDAY

NOTES

*W*eekly
SCHEDULE
PLANNER

MONDAY

TUESDAY

MONTH

WEEK NO.

WEDNESDAY

THURSDAY

FRIDAY

SATURDAY

SUNDAY

NOTES

Weekly
SCHEDULE
PLANNER

MONDAY

TUESDAY

MONTH

WEEK NO.

WEDNESDAY

THURSDAY

FRIDAY

SATURDAY

SUNDAY

NOTES

Weekly
SCHEDULE
PLANNER

MONDAY

TUESDAY

MONTH

WEEK NO.

WEDNESDAY

THURSDAY

FRIDAY

SATURDAY

SUNDAY

NOTES

How are You doing?

Mind:

_____
_____
_____
_____
_____

Body:

_____
_____
_____
_____
_____
_____

Money:

_____
_____
_____
_____
_____
_____
_____

Set Your Intentions:

_____
_____
_____
_____
_____
_____

Journaled
Thoughts...

_____

_____

_____

_____

_____

_____

_____

_____

_____

_____

_____

_____

_____

_____

_____

_____

_____

_____

_____

_____

_____

_____

_____

_____

Goals for the Month

Month: _____

Weekly
SCHEDULE
PLANNER

MONDAY

TUESDAY

MONTH

WEEK NO.

WEDNESDAY

THURSDAY

FRIDAY

SATURDAY

SUNDAY

NOTES

Weekly
SCHEDULE
PLANNER

MONDAY

TUESDAY

MONTH

WEEK NO.

WEDNESDAY

THURSDAY

FRIDAY

SATURDAY

SUNDAY

NOTES

*W*eekly
SCHEDULE
PLANNER

MONTH

WEEK NO.

MONDAY

TUESDAY

WEDNESDAY

THURSDAY

FRIDAY

SATURDAY

SUNDAY

NOTES

Weekly SCHEDULE PLANNER

MONDAY

TUESDAY

MONTH

WEEK NO.

WEDNESDAY

THURSDAY

FRIDAY

SATURDAY

SUNDAY

NOTES

Weekly
SCHEDULE
PLANNER

MONTH

WEEK NO.

MONDAY

TUESDAY

WEDNESDAY

THURSDAY

FRIDAY

SATURDAY

SUNDAY

NOTES

How are You doing?

Mind:

_____
_____
_____
_____
_____

Body:

_____
_____
_____
_____
_____
_____
_____

Money:

_____
_____
_____
_____
_____
_____
_____

Set Your Intentions:

_____
_____
_____
_____
_____
_____
_____

Journaled
Thoughts...

Accomplished
Goals for the
previous Quarter

Quarter/Year: _____

The Entrepreneur's

Success
Journal

Be excellent!

- Deliver great service/products!
- Be respectful to everyone. (Respectful doesn't mean be a pushover.)
- Keep your word!
- Listen to your customer feedback where applicable.
- Share what your customers have to say if need be.
- Partner with other people of excellence.
- Be accountable, accept responsibility and apologize if needed.
- Pay your fees, taxes and licenses on time!
- Reach out for help from experts when needed. Growth calls for it. You shouldn't do everything on your own...forever.

Breathe:

Intro:

This breathing technique uses imagery or focus words/phrases.You can choose a focus word that makes you smile, feel relaxed, or that is simply neutral to think about. Example: "peace, let go, or relax", but can be any word that suits you to focus on & repeat through your practice.As you build up your breath focus practice you can start with a 10-minute session.

Introspect:

Notice how you feel at the end of the exercise.

Instructions:

1. Sit or lie down in a comfortable place.
2. Place one hand below your belly button, keeping your belly relaxed, and notice how it rises with each inhale and falls with each exhale.
3. Let out a loud sigh with each exhale.
4. Begin the practice of breath focus by combining this deep breathing with imagery and a focus word or phrase that will support relaxation.
5. You can imagine that the air you inhale brings waves of peace and calm throughout your body. Mentally say, "Inhaling peace and calm."
6. Imagine that the air you exhale washes away tension and anxiety. You can say to yourself, "Exhaling tension and anxiety."

Goal Setting for
_____ Quarter

What are 3 areas that you want to grow in personally?

_____
_____
_____
_____
_____
_____
_____
_____
_____

What is your end goal for all three goals?

_____
_____
_____
_____
_____
_____
_____

How committed are you to your goals?

_____
_____
_____
_____
_____
_____

1st Goal

_____

Steps to achieving my Goal   **Priorities**

Quote of the Day

"The secret to success is to learn to accept the impossible, to do without the indispensable, and to bear the intolerable."
– Nelson Mandela

2nd Goal

_____

Steps to achieving my Goal   **Priorities**

Quote of the Day

_"Most people search high and wide for
the key to success. If they only knew the
key to their dreams lies within."
– George Washington Carver_

3rd Goal

Steps to achieving my Goal   **Priorities**

Quote of the Day

"In the darkest moments I can still find peace."
– Marian Anderson

 **Business Goals for ____ Quarter**

Month:_____

Marketing: How much time and money will you invest?

Followup: What customers and partners do you need to reachout to?

Tasks: What are the tasks you are avoiding but need to get done?

Complete: What did you finish this quarter? (Roll any unfinished task to next quarter.)

Weekly
SCHEDULE
PLANNER

MONDAY

TUESDAY

MONTH

WEEK NO.

WEDNESDAY

THURSDAY

FRIDAY

SATURDAY

SUNDAY

NOTES

Weekly
SCHEDULE
PLANNER

MONTH

WEEK NO.

MONDAY	TUESDAY

WEDNESDAY	THURSDAY	FRIDAY

SATURDAY	SUNDAY	NOTES

Weekly
SCHEDULE
PLANNER

MONTH

WEEK NO.

MONDAY

TUESDAY

WEDNESDAY

THURSDAY

FRIDAY

SATURDAY

SUNDAY

NOTES

Weekly
SCHEDULE
PLANNER

MONDAY

TUESDAY

MONTH

WEEK NO.

WEDNESDAY

THURSDAY

FRIDAY

SATURDAY

SUNDAY

NOTES

*W*eekly
SCHEDULE
PLANNER

MONTH

WEEK NO.

MONDAY

TUESDAY

WEDNESDAY

THURSDAY

FRIDAY

SATURDAY

SUNDAY

NOTES

How are You doing?

Mind:
_____
_____
_____
_____
_____

Body:
_____
_____
_____
_____
_____
_____

Money:
_____
_____
_____
_____
_____
_____

Set Your Intentions:
_____
_____
_____
_____
_____
_____

Journaled
Thoughts...

_____
_____
_____
_____
_____
_____
_____
_____
_____
_____
_____
_____
_____
_____
_____
_____
_____
_____
_____
_____
_____
_____
_____
_____
_____
_____
_____
_____

Accomplished

Goals for the Month

Month: _____

_____
_____
_____
_____
_____
_____
_____
_____
_____
_____
_____
_____
_____
_____
_____
_____
_____
_____
_____
_____
_____
_____
_____
_____
_____
_____
_____
_____
_____
_____

Weekly
SCHEDULE
PLANNER

MONDAY

TUESDAY

MONTH

WEEK NO.

WEDNESDAY

THURSDAY

FRIDAY

SATURDAY

SUNDAY

NOTES

Weekly
SCHEDULE
PLANNER

MONDAY

TUESDAY

MONTH

WEEK NO.

WEDNESDAY

THURSDAY

FRIDAY

SATURDAY

SUNDAY

NOTES

Weekly
SCHEDULE
PLANNER

MONTH

WEEK NO.

MONDAY

TUESDAY

WEDNESDAY

THURSDAY

FRIDAY

SATURDAY

SUNDAY

NOTES

*W*eekly
SCHEDULE
PLANNER

MONTH

WEEK NO.

MONDAY

TUESDAY

WEDNESDAY

THURSDAY

FRIDAY

SATURDAY

SUNDAY

NOTES

Weekly
SCHEDULE
PLANNER

MONDAY

TUESDAY

MONTH

WEEK NO.

WEDNESDAY

THURSDAY

FRIDAY

SATURDAY

SUNDAY

NOTES

How are You doing?

Mind:
_____
_____
_____
_____
_____

Body:
_____
_____
_____
_____
_____
_____
_____

Money:
_____
_____
_____
_____
_____
_____
_____

Set Your Intentions:
_____
_____
_____
_____
_____
_____

Journaled

Thoughts...

Accomplished

Goals for the Month

Month: _____

_____
_____
_____
_____
_____
_____
_____
_____
_____
_____
_____
_____
_____
_____
_____
_____
_____
_____
_____
_____
_____
_____
_____
_____
_____
_____
_____
_____
_____
_____

Weekly
SCHEDULE
PLANNER

MONDAY

TUESDAY

MONTH

WEEK NO.

WEDNESDAY

THURSDAY

FRIDAY

SATURDAY

SUNDAY

NOTES

Weekly
SCHEDULE
PLANNER

MONDAY

TUESDAY

MONTH

WEEK NO.

WEDNESDAY

THURSDAY

FRIDAY

SATURDAY

SUNDAY

NOTES

Weekly
SCHEDULE
PLANNER

MONTH

WEEK NO.

MONDAY	TUESDAY

WEDNESDAY	THURSDAY	FRIDAY

SATURDAY	SUNDAY	NOTES

*W*eekly
SCHEDULE
PLANNER

MONDAY

TUESDAY

MONTH

WEEK NO.

WEDNESDAY

THURSDAY

FRIDAY

SATURDAY

SUNDAY

NOTES

How are You doing?

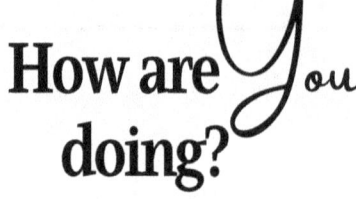

Mind:

_____
_____
_____
_____
_____

Body:

_____
_____
_____
_____
_____
_____
_____

Money:

_____
_____
_____
_____
_____
_____
_____

Set Your Intentions:

_____
_____
_____
_____
_____
_____

Journaled
Thoughts...

_____
_____
_____
_____
_____
_____
_____
_____
_____
_____
_____
_____
_____
_____
_____
_____
_____
_____
_____
_____
_____
_____
_____
_____
_____
_____
_____
_____
_____

Accomplished
Goals for the
previous Quarter

Quarter/Year: _____

_____
_____
_____
_____
_____
_____
_____
_____
_____
_____
_____
_____
_____
_____
_____
_____
_____
_____
_____
_____
_____
_____
_____
_____
_____
_____
_____
_____
_____
_____
_____

The
Entrepreneur's
Success
Journal

Patience is not a punishment!

Patience is a super vitamin.
As an entrepreneur , patience is one of the
most needed qualities... patience with yourself,
your ideas, your team, family and friends,
marketing, process and journey all together!
Your efforts are not in vain and may not yield
and automatic return, but will show its value
at some point. Don't dismiss your seed because
you don't see the fruit right away. And don't
allow the frustration of anxiousness to
paralyze your efforts either. Keep working!
You got this!

Breathe:

Intro:

Please try the 4–7–8 Breathing technique when you are feeling an onset of anxiety episodes.
Find a place to sit down with your back straight and the tip of your tongue on the back of your upper front teeth.
Please note that this technique can be used at any time.

Introspect:

Notice how you feel at the end of the exercise.

Instructions:

1. Breathe out through the mouth, making a whooshing sound.
2. Close the mouth and count to 4 while breathing in through the nose.
3. Count to 7 while holding the breath.
4. Count to 8 while breathing out through the mouth, making a whooshing sound.
5. Inhale, then repeat three times.

Goal Setting for
_____ Quarter

What are 3 areas that you want to grow in personally?

_____
_____
_____
_____
_____
_____
_____
_____
_____

What is your end goal for all three goals?

_____
_____
_____
_____
_____
_____
_____

How committed are you to your goals?

_____
_____
_____
_____
_____
_____
_____
_____

1st Goal

_____

Steps to achieving my Goal   **Priorities**

Quote of the Day

"Remember, it's the little things that count."
– George Johnson

2nd Goal

_____

Steps to achieving my Goal   **Priorities**

Quote of the Day

"The future is purchased by the present."
– Daisy Lee Bates

3rd Goal

Steps to achieving my Goal   **Priorities**

Quote of the Day

"Some people succeed because they are destined to, but most people succeed because they are determined to."
– Roscoe Dunjee

Business Goals
for _____ Quarter

Month:_____

Marketing: How much time and money will you invest?

Followup: What customers and partners do you need to reachout to?

Tasks: What are the tasks you are avoiding but need to get done?

Complete: What did you finish this quarter? (Roll any unfinished task to next quarter.)

Weekly
SCHEDULE
PLANNER

MONDAY

TUESDAY

MONTH

WEEK NO.

WEDNESDAY

THURSDAY

FRIDAY

SATURDAY

SUNDAY

NOTES

*W*eekly
SCHEDULE
PLANNER

MONDAY

TUESDAY

MONTH

WEEK NO.

WEDNESDAY

THURSDAY

FRIDAY

SATURDAY

SUNDAY

NOTES

Weekly
SCHEDULE
PLANNER

MONDAY

TUESDAY

MONTH

WEEK NO.

WEDNESDAY

THURSDAY

FRIDAY

SATURDAY

SUNDAY

NOTES

Weekly
SCHEDULE
PLANNER

MONTH

WEEK NO.

MONDAY

TUESDAY

WEDNESDAY

THURSDAY

FRIDAY

SATURDAY

SUNDAY

NOTES

Weekly
SCHEDULE
PLANNER

MONTH

WEEK NO.

MONDAY

TUESDAY

WEDNESDAY

THURSDAY

FRIDAY

SATURDAY

SUNDAY

NOTES

How are You doing?

Mind:

_____
_____
_____
_____
_____

Body:

_____
_____
_____
_____
_____
_____

Money:

_____
_____
_____
_____
_____
_____

Set Your Intentions:

_____
_____
_____
_____
_____
_____

Journaled
Thoughts...

Accomplished
Goals for the
previous Quarter

Quarter/Year: _____

_____
_____
_____
_____
_____
_____
_____
_____
_____
_____
_____
_____
_____
_____
_____
_____
_____
_____
_____
_____
_____
_____
_____
_____
_____
_____
_____
_____
_____
_____
_____
_____

Weekly
SCHEDULE
PLANNER

MONTH

WEEK NO.

MONDAY

TUESDAY

WEDNESDAY

THURSDAY

FRIDAY

SATURDAY

SUNDAY

NOTES

Weekly
SCHEDULE
PLANNER

MONTH

WEEK NO.

MONDAY

TUESDAY

WEDNESDAY

THURSDAY

FRIDAY

SATURDAY

SUNDAY

NOTES

Weekly
SCHEDULE
PLANNER

MONTH

WEEK NO.

MONDAY

TUESDAY

WEDNESDAY

THURSDAY

FRIDAY

SATURDAY

SUNDAY

NOTES

Weekly
SCHEDULE
PLANNER

MONTH

WEEK NO.

MONDAY

TUESDAY

WEDNESDAY

THURSDAY

FRIDAY

SATURDAY

SUNDAY

NOTES

Weekly
SCHEDULE
PLANNER

MONDAY

TUESDAY

MONTH

WEEK NO.

WEDNESDAY

THURSDAY

FRIDAY

SATURDAY

SUNDAY

NOTES

How are You doing?

Mind:

_____
_____
_____
_____
_____

Body:

_____
_____
_____
_____
_____
_____

Money:

_____
_____
_____
_____
_____
_____

Set Your Intentions:

_____
_____
_____
_____
_____
_____

Journaled
Thoughts...

Goals for the Month

Month: _____

_____
_____
_____
_____
_____
_____
_____
_____
_____
_____
_____
_____
_____
_____
_____
_____
_____
_____
_____
_____
_____
_____
_____
_____
_____
_____
_____
_____

Weekly
SCHEDULE
PLANNER

MONTH

WEEK NO.

MONDAY

TUESDAY

WEDNESDAY

THURSDAY

FRIDAY

SATURDAY

SUNDAY

NOTES

*W*eekly
SCHEDULE
PLANNER

MONDAY

TUESDAY

MONTH

WEEK NO.

WEDNESDAY

THURSDAY

FRIDAY

SATURDAY

SUNDAY

NOTES

Weekly
SCHEDULE
PLANNER

MONDAY

TUESDAY

MONTH

WEEK NO.

WEDNESDAY

THURSDAY

FRIDAY

SATURDAY

SUNDAY

NOTES

Weekly
SCHEDULE
PLANNER

MONTH

WEEK NO.

MONDAY

TUESDAY

WEDNESDAY

THURSDAY

FRIDAY

SATURDAY

SUNDAY

NOTES

Weekly
SCHEDULE
PLANNER

MONTH

WEEK NO.

MONDAY

TUESDAY

WEDNESDAY

THURSDAY

FRIDAY

SATURDAY

SUNDAY

NOTES

How are You doing?

Mind:

_____
_____
_____
_____

Body:

_____
_____
_____
_____
_____
_____

Money:

_____
_____
_____
_____
_____
_____

Set Your Intentions:

_____
_____
_____
_____
_____
_____

Journaled
Thoughts...

Accomplished
Goals for the
previous Quarter

Quarter/Year: _____

_____
_____
_____
_____
_____
_____
_____
_____
_____
_____
_____
_____
_____
_____
_____
_____
_____
_____
_____
_____
_____
_____
_____
_____
_____
_____
_____
_____

The
Entrepreneur's
Success
Journal

Protect your assets!

Are you making sure you are maximizing your dollar by saving, investing, and insuring what you value?

- Make sure you have insurance for your business to protect you, your family, assets. Also cover your customers if needed.
- Make sure you save money that you make. You never know what the future holds and want to be able to maintain if a major event happens.
- Make sure you have "Desk Instructions" incase you are unable to do your part, can someone else fill your shoes and keep the flow of your business?

www.ingramcontent.com/pod-product-compliance
Lightning Source LLC
Chambersburg PA
CBHW080835220526
45467CB00008B/2283